D0604863

MONTANA BRANCH
Santa Monica Public Library

AUG. – –2015

BACKYARD ANIMALS
AMERICAN CROWS
by Kristin Petrie

**Checkerboard
Library**
An Imprint of Abdo Publishing
www.abdopublishing.com

www.abdopublishing.com

Published by Abdo Publishing, a division of ABDO, PO Box 398166, Minneapolis, Minnesota 55439.
Copyright © 2015 by Abdo Consulting Group, Inc. International copyrights reserved in all countries. No part of this book may be reproduced in any form without written permission from the publisher. Checkerboard Library™ is a trademark and logo of Abdo Publishing.

Printed in the United States of America, North Mankato, Minnesota.
102014
012015

THIS BOOK CONTAINS
RECYCLED MATERIALS

Cover Photos: iStockphoto, Science Source
Interior Photos: Alamy pp. 9, 11, 19, 23; Glow Images pp. 1, 15, 27, 29; JOEL SARTORE/National Geographic
   Creative p. 5; ROBBIE GEORGE/National Geographic Creative p. 25; Science Source pp. 13, 16–17, 21, 23, 26

Series Coordinator: Megan M. Gunderson
Editors: Rochelle Baltzer, Bridget O'Brien
Art Direction: Neil Klinepier

Library of Congress Cataloging-in-Publication Data

Petrie, Kristin, 1970- author.
  American crows / Kristin Petrie.
     pages cm. -- (Backyard animals)
  Audience: Ages 8-12.
  Includes index.
  ISBN 978-1-62403-658-3
1. Corvus brachyrhynchos--Juvenile literature. 2. Crows--Juvenile literature. I. Title.
  QL696.P2367P48 2015
  598.8'64--dc23
                    2014024347

TABLE OF CONTENTS

THE BIRD FAMILY

Birds! Birds are everywhere. They come in many shapes and sizes. Some are beautiful, while others are considered downright ugly. They nest in trees and on the ground. They have webbed feet or feature sharp **talons**. Some birds waddle clumsily, rarely leaving the ground. Others fly with speed and grace.

Despite their many differences, all birds belong to the class Aves. Within this group, over half of all birds are part of the scientific order Passeriformes. Members of this large order are songbirds. These land birds have unwebbed toes for perching.

The order Passeriformes is made up of numerous bird families. The family Corvidae, for example, includes more than 100 types of birds. Jays, magpies, ravens, rooks, coughs, nutcrackers, and crows are all corvids. One species from the family Corvidae is very widespread. Can you guess what it is? It is the American crow!

SCIENTIFIC CLASSIFICATION

Kingdom: Animalia
Phylum: Chordata
Class: Aves
Order: Passeriformes
Family: Corvidae
Genus: *Corvus*
Species: *brachyrhynchos*

The American crow is just one of the more than 10,000 species in the class Aves.

CROWS

The American crow is just one crow species. Crows are widespread and live around the world. In fact, the only places crows do not live have extreme cold. These include the North Pole, southern South America, and Antarctica. Some crows also avoid deserts.

The United States is home to several crow species. The crow you may be most familiar with is *Corvus brachyrhynchos*, or the American crow. These birds are such a frequent sight that they are also called common crows.

American crows are dark, bold, and **inquisitive**. They have excellent senses of sight and smell, and they have great memories. American crows hang out in large groups, often becoming a **nuisance**. Plus, many of these birds do not **migrate**. So, they are present year-round.

American crows like to spend their time in a wide variety of settings. These include crop fields, dumpsters, campsites, city streets, and backyards. They're everywhere!

MANY NAMES

In French, the American crow is known as the *corneille d'Amérique*. In Spanish, it is the *cuervo americano*.

Canada

United States

Mexico

Where American Crows Live

N

North
America

Europe

Asia

Africa

South
America

Australia

HABITAT

The American crow is native to North America. It is found across the **Nearctic** region. American crows live in southern Canada and across the continental United States.

Crows are hardy birds. They have adapted to many climates and **environments**. The American crow population grew as settlers moved west across the United States. Crows like grasslands, fields of grains, and trees. But they don't like endless forests. So, the spread of agriculture opened land and helped the population spread.

As people occupied more and more land, crows also adapted to **urban** life. Today, crows are a common sight among humans and their supply of delicious food.

Despite their increasing presence in cities, crows are still drawn to large open areas. These areas allow for ground **foraging** and for large flocks to assemble. Playgrounds, ball fields, and parking lots will do, as long as there is food and a place to rest. Crows also live on coasts.

Crows enjoy agricultural and grassland areas that have forest edges nearby. This combination gives them places for foraging, roosting, and brooding.

BILL TO TAIL

Male and female American crows look the same. They are black. This dark color theme includes their long, strong legs and grasping toes. This species has brown eyes, a thick neck, and a large, slightly hooked bill. Stiff **bristles** cover the nostrils.

The American crow is the largest crow in North America. It ranges from 15.7 to 20.9 inches (39.9 to 53.1 cm) long. The bird's wide wingspan doubles this measure at 33.5 to 39.4 inches (85.1 to 100.1 cm)! Most American crows weigh around one pound (0.5 kg). Only about 20 percent of males are larger than females.

The American crow's coat of feathers is glossy black and slightly **iridescent** with a purplish tint. It refreshes itself with an annual **molt**. Young crows get brown and ragged-looking during their first winter before their first molt in the spring. Crows don't lose all of their feathers at once. The feathers are replaced one at a time as they regrow.

When flying, American crows show off fingerlike flight feathers. The tail is fan-shaped with a rounded or squared-off end.

HOP!
American crows use their strong legs to hop on the ground. One foot hits the ground just before the other.

THE AMERICAN CROW

WING

HEAD

EYE

BILL

TAIL

FEET

WING

SIMILAR SPECIES

American crows are similar in appearance to several other birds. Fish crows are nearly identical to American crows. Fish crows are slightly smaller than their American crow relatives. Fish crows are 14 to 16 inches (36 to 41 cm) long and have a more **nasal** call. Unlike on the American crow, it is hard to see individual feathers on a fish crow's back.

The northwestern crow is also similar to the American crow. It has a more hoarse call. And, it is smaller and more slender. The northwestern crow measures 16 to 17 inches (41 to 43 cm) long. This species lives only on the Pacific coast from Alaska to Washington.

Lastly, the common raven is frequently confused with the American crow. Ravens are much larger, weighing 2 to 4 pounds (0.8 to 1.8 kg). They measure 17 to 24 inches (43 to 61 cm) long. Unlike the American crow's squared-off tail, the raven's tail comes to a point. And, its heavy bill is larger than the American crow's.

An American crow

A common raven

SMART & SOCIAL

Many people find American crows intriguing. Crows are highly social and very intelligent. Yet other people dislike these birds. American crows can be mischievous and **aggressive** when there is something they want. And, they sometimes gather in large groups!

American and other crow species have complex social systems. There are three main types of social groups. The first is the family group. Crow family groups are generally up to 15 members in size. Families include a breeding pair and offspring from previous years.

Interestingly, crows are cooperative breeders. Cooperative breeders stay together for long periods. They share the job of raising and protecting the family group.

Some offspring of these mates are born into a helper role. Helper crows do not attempt to find mates. Rather, they "cooperate" to help the family meet its needs. They help raise the young. And, they defend the family's year-round home territory. Crows may join larger flocks during the day for **foraging** and then return to their families at night.

YOU DON'T SAY!
Crow's-feet are the wrinkles at the sides of someone's eyes. A crow's nest is a platform high up on a ship's mast that lets sailors see far.

An American crow
preening itself. Members
of a family group also
preen one another, which
is called allopreening.

Sometimes, American crows form massive groups. For example in winter **roosting**, crows may gather near large trees in the late afternoon. These groups then roost together for the night. Many of these large flocks return to the same winter roosting site year after year. Some flocks include more than 1 million birds!

Crows learn from each other. This includes where to find food and how to avoid dangers.

Another type of crow group is a floater flock. These crows roam together to find mates and establish new territories. Being in a group makes this safer.

No matter what size the flock, crows work together. American crows figure out how to solve problems and defend territory and one another. One interesting method of defense is called mobbing. In mobbing, a group of crows vocally harasses and chases a predator to scare or distract it.

This can include people! American crows are so smart that they recognize individual human faces. If someone does something to threaten a crow in some way, the crow will remember that person. And, it will communicate to other crows that the person is an enemy. So when the person shows up again, many crows may dive-bomb and harass him!

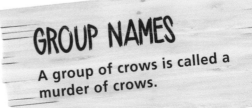

GROUP NAMES

A group of crows is called a murder of crows.

COMMUNICATION

What does the crow say? Caw caw! In reality, the American crow uses more than 20 calls. Mobbing starts with harsh, loud cawing. Longer caws say, "Get off my land!" Alarm calls may sound more like "kos kos!" Still other caws are simple conversations between neighbors and family members. Very young crows communicate in high-pitched, **nasal** voices.

American crows also sing. These songs are several minutes long. Crow songs consist of soft, low caws, clicking noises, and throaty coos. They are often used with family and may be for greeting and bonding. Unlike many other birds, male and female American crows sing the same songs.

An American crow's songs may not be sweet like a robin's, but they are still considered songs.

NESTING

American crows build their nests annually in the spring. Crows prefer pine trees for their nests, but they will use **deciduous** trees if needed. Nests are typically built in the top third of a tree. They can be 6 to 60 feet (2 to 18 m) off the ground.

Crows build their nests in a space near the trunk or on a branch. What if there are no trees, such as in some city areas? Crows can nest on buildings and even telephone poles.

Building the nest is a family affair. The breeding pair and sometimes young from past years work together on the new home. Crows form the outside of their nests with medium-sized branches and twigs. Soft debris such as pine needles, weeds, soft bark, and animal hair lines a nest's interior.

Nest size varies greatly. Nests typically range from 6 to 19 inches (15 to 48 cm) wide and 4 to 15 inches (10 to 38 cm) deep. The base can be 2 feet (0.6 m) wide and 1 foot (0.3 m) thick. Building a nest takes 5 to 13 days.

People do not often see a crow's courtship behavior. However, it involves aerial displays, dancing, bowing, and a rattle-type song. Crows also strut, with their wings and tail spread and coat puffed up. After mating, the female crow is ready to lay her eggs.

American crows
usually mate for life.

BABY CROWS

The female crow lays a **clutch** of three to nine bluish-green to olive-green eggs. The eggs have brown and gray spots, especially near the larger end.

The female crow **incubates** her eggs for 16 to 18 days. The male crow and other helpers assist her during this time. They feed her and protect her.

Hatchlings are born with tufts of grayish **down** on wrinkly skin. They are almost bald. They have blue eyes at birth, but at first their eyes are closed.

The hatchlings grow quickly, but they remain in the nest for 20 to 40 days. Their parents feed them many times a day. After this time, young crows can fly and begin exploring. They follow the male and female crows to learn how to **forage**.

Many young crows stay near the family nest for several more years. There can be young crows from five different years in the group of up to 15 birds. During this time, they act as helpers to the breeding pair. Crows that leave their family begin breeding between 2 and 4 years of age.

Common crow eggs are 1.4 to 1.9 inches (3.6 to 4.7 cm) long.

For the first year, a crow's mouth is bright red.

HOW OLD?
The oldest crow in the wild lived to be 16 years old. In captivity, the oldest crow reached the age of 59!

DIET

What do crows eat? It may be easier to answer what they do not eat! Crows are omnivores, and they eat just about anything. They are also opportunistic feeders, eating whenever food is available. Crows regularly stash extra food in **caches**. These hiding places can be in tree crevices or on the ground covered up with plant material.

Flocks of crows feast on grains, fruits, seeds, and nuts. They eat small critters such as mice, frogs, rabbits, turtles, fish, and other amphibians and reptiles. They will also eat other birds' eggs and **nestlings**. They rarely eat from bird feeders. But, crows are known for their love of garbage, dog food, people food, and roadkill!

Crows mainly **forage** for food on the ground. However, they are very crafty in their pursuit of something tasty. Crows spy on other birds to find their hidden nests, eggs, and food. Gangs of crows also harass and distract animals and people. Then, one of their members snatches the person's lunch!

Can't open that nut? That's no problem for the intelligent crow. It will hold a nut with one foot while cracking it open with its bill. American crows also drop clams and mussels from high up onto hard surfaces to crack them open.

Crows love water! They are frequent visitors to birdbaths, puddles, and ponds. In addition, crows dip dry foods in water. Soft food is much easier than hard food for crows to eat. After a long sip, crows are likely to jump in and take a bath!

Crows need to eat about 11 ounces (300 g) of food each day.

ENEMIES & CHALLENGES

Crows aren't just predators. They are also prey. Despite a family's cooperative efforts to protect and raise their young, many crows die before birth or as **fledglings**. Nearly 50 percent are lost to predators or natural causes.

Crow predators include other birds, such as red-tailed hawks and the great horned owl. Sneaky creatures such as snakes, house cats, and raccoons are also a threat. Crows use numerous methods, such as cawing alerts and mobbing, to try to defend themselves and others.

In addition, crows are prey for humans. Crows are considered small game, and crow hunting is legal in open seasons. Numerous laws

Crows are so intelligent that they are hard for researchers to capture for study!

regulate crow hunting. This includes the size of firearms, hours of the day when shooting is allowed, and length of the hunting season. However, crow hunting is not legal in every state.

Crows are attracted to shiny objects, such as keys.

CROWS & HUMANS

Besides hunting for sport, humans have attempted to decrease the crow population for economic reasons. Huge flocks of crows descend upon and eat a good share of crops. Farmers first dealt with this problem by placing a fake person, or scarecrow, in their fields. Since crows are very intelligent, this did not work for long.

Luckily, crows also help farmers. They eat insect pests on crops. And when crows **forage**, they also disperse seeds. This helps growers of all kinds. On the other hand, crow droppings near human populations are a concern for disease.

Crows also face disease. The West Nile virus has greatly affected several crow populations. For uncertain reasons, crows are highly **susceptible** to this disease. Those that acquire it die within days. Luckily, the American crow population remains stable. The **IUCN** considers them "least concern" because their population is large and generally increasing, and they have a large range.

Crows have relatively large brains. They can count, solve problems, and remember thousands of food stashes. Crows also **mimic** the sounds of other birds as well as human voices, especially in captivity. However, crows are illegal to keep as pets. So, people must admire their talents from afar!

In some cultures, crows symbolize death or are a sign of something bad to come. In others, they are seen as wise.

GLOSSARY

aggressive (uh-GREH-sihv) - displaying hostility.

bristle (BRIH-suhl) - a short, stiff hair.

cache (KASH) - a secure or hidden place in which to store something. Something stored in such a place can also be called a cache.

clutch - a nest of eggs.

deciduous (dih-SIH-juh-wuhs) - shedding leaves each year. Deciduous forests have trees or shrubs that do this.

down - soft, fluffy feathers.

environment - all the surroundings that affect the growth and well-being of a living thing.

fledgling - a young bird that has gained its feathers and can leave the nest.

forage - to search.

hatchling - a bird that has recently hatched.

incubate - to keep eggs warm, often by sitting on them, so they will hatch.

inquisitive - tending to investigate or seek knowledge.

iridescent (ihr-uh-DEHS-uhnt) - shining with many different colors when viewed from different angles.

IUCN - the International Union for Conservation of Nature. The IUCN is a global environmental organization focused on conservation.

migrate - to move from one place to another, often to find food.

mimic - to imitate or copy.

molt - to shed skin, hair, or feathers and replace with new growth.

nasal - sound made by pushing air out through the nose when speaking.

Nearctic - a geographic region that includes Greenland and North America to northern Mexico.

nestling - a young bird that cannot yet leave the nest.

nuisance (NOO-suhnts) - something that is annoying or causes trouble.

roost - to perch or settle down to rest. A roost is a place, such as a cave or a tree, where animals rest.

susceptible (suh-SEHP-tuh-buhl) - having little resistance.

talon - a claw, especially of a bird of prey.

urban - of or relating to a city.

WEBSITES

To learn more about Backyard Animals,
visit **booklinks.abdopublishing.com**. These links are routinely
monitored and updated to provide the most current information available.

INDEX